Narcissist

How To Beat The Narcissist!

Understanding Narcissism &

Narcissistic Personality

Disorder

Jane Aniston

Table of Contents

Introduction

Chapter 1. Narcissus and Echo

Chapter 2. What Makes a Narcissist?

9 Traits of the Narcissist

Narcissist vs. NPD

Causes of Narcissism

Covert and Overt Narcissism

Is there an epidemic?

Chapter 3. The Narcissist's Drug & Greatest Fear

Narcissistic Supply

Primary

Secondary

Narcissist's Injury

Narcissist's Rage

Chapter 4.Spotting the Narcissist

On a Date

The Narcissistic Friend

In the Family

The Narcissistic Parent

The Narcissistic Spouse

At Work

The Narcissistic Boss

The Narcissistic Co-worker

On the Internet

On Facebook

Chapter 5. Dealing with or Getting Away from the Narcissist

Knowing the Narcissist's Mind Games

Tools to Get Away

Chapter 6. Quotes To Help You Better Understand The Narcissist

Conclusion

A message from the author, Jane Aniston

<u>Introduction</u>

Narcissism is a hot topic nowadays. Some people say that society is becoming more and more narcissistic. Is the present preoccupation with selfies proof of our increasing narcissism and is the Internet to blame? Is narcissism always a bad thing? Can a narcissist be a productive and valued member of society? Are all narcissists dangerous and heartless? What causes narcissism?

Although we know that a narcissist is a person who has an inflated sense of self, there are many things we need to learn about narcissism. Who is a narcissist? How can you tell if a person is a narcissist? Why do people get trapped in relationships with narcissists and how can they get away? Is a narcissist the same as a person with Narcissistic Personality Disorder (NPD)?

There is so much to know about narcissism. This book will try to explain things in simple terms. If you don't want to sift through all the medical jargon and you just want to understand narcissism in plain English, this is for you.

Why is it important to understand narcissism? You may be in a relationship with a narcissist and not know it. Knowing how to spot one and what to do about it can relieve you of much anguish.

Understanding narcissism will help prevent you from falling into the narcissist's trap and help you to cope with the narcissists you have to deal with. Learning to deal with narcissists can empower you. This book hopes to help you break free if you are in the narcissist's hold and find strength in yourself.

Chapter 1

Narcissus and Echo

It's interesting how seemingly innocent children's stories, fairytales or fables can speak universal truths and help us understand complex psychological conditions. Greek mythology has always been interesting and entertaining to many and the story of Narcissus is a fascinating tale from which narcissism got its name. There are many versions of this story but let me tell it to you as I remember it.

It's a story of a handsome young youth by the name of Narcissus. When Narcissus was born, his mother brought him to the blind prophet Tiresias and asked if her son would live long. Tiresias replied: "He'll have a long life as long as he never knows himself."

When Narcissus grew older, his good looks attracted many- mortal and immortal alike. Nymphs and fairies followed him everywhere he went, trying to win his heart and attention. But Narcissus paid no attention to them and simply went about his hunting duties.

Among the wood nymphs and fairies who were crazy about Narcissus was Echo. Echo was a very talkative wood nymph and this somehow didn't sit well with the goddess Hera. Hera was so piqued, it seemed, with Echo's long-windedness, that she placed a curse on the hapless wood-nymph. Poor Echo would no longer be able to say what was on her mind but was doomed to simply repeat whatever was spoken to her. So, Echo could not express her love for the very fetching and charming Narcissus. She continued to stalk him, however, and believed she could still find a way to let him know of her undying love for him.

It is said that, once, Narcissus sensed he was being followed and called out to whoever was there. Of course, Echo could only repeat his words. When he did see her, he was unimpressed and even somewhat repulsed. Echo was clearly beautiful and beguiling but she didn't seem to be his type. She continued to pursue him, however, waiting for the right moment to finally let him know how she felt for him.

Remember, it wasn't only Echo who was smitten by Narcissus. Many others were infatuated with his good looks, but Narcissus rejected them all. Narcissus seemed incapable of falling in love at that time. This soon came to the ears of Nemesis, the goddess of divine retribution. Some call her the goddess of vengeance. A rejected lover had purportedly asked Nemesis to never let Narcissus be loved in return.

In one of his hunting trips, Narcissus gets thirsty and looks around for a place to get a drink. He comes upon a pond and crouches down to drink water. This is the moment that Narcissus glimpses his reflection in the mirror-clear water and promptly falls in love with himself. Some people say the water was enchanted and that it had cast its spell on Narcissus, making him unable to get away.

Narcissus is completely unaware that he has fallen madly in love with his own image in the water. He tries to speak to it, to ask questions. At this point, Echo, who is still lurking about, thinks she has found the opportunity to tell him her feelings. Whenever Narcissus says "I love you" to his reflection, Echo repeats it back to him. But Narcissus is still oblivious to Echo and is hopelessly enamored with his reflection. He tries hard to get some kind of response from his reflection and refuses to leave the side of the pond. There he stays, simply gazing at himself, perhaps hoping to get some kind of requital from his image; fantasizing until he eventually weakens and dies. Others say he tries to reach for his reflection and drowns in the pond; others say he committed suicide.

Soon after, where Narcissus once crouched gazing at himself, the plant named after him first sprung up, with beautiful flowers gazing down at the water. Echo, on the other hand, still pined for him even though he was already gone. She soon wasted away, fading until only her voice remained in the mountains.

This story is filled with insights on self-love and how it affects people around you. Echo is sometimes forgotten when this story is retold, but the significance of her role in the narcissist's web should not be overlooked.

Clearly, Narcissus turned away everyone who tried to have some degree of intimacy with him. He rejected them because they loved him, and he was incapable of love at that time. When he did fall in love, it was with an image – an illusion. And, it was with himself. Similarly, the person who tries to establish a relationship with the narcissist may only be able to do so if he or she is willing to simply reflect the narcissist's own views. If you want to get the narcissist attention, you must simply echo his ideas and opinions, you must be in total agreement with him. Just like Echo, your voice or opinion may be reduced simply to a repetition of the narcissist's. And your identity will be reduced to a mist, a whisper devoid of body or personality.

The narcissist is unaware of how much he adores himself and he is most likely unaware of how he can ruin lives. He may be aware but he doesn't care. Like Narcissus in the story, he may not know his true self.

He may only know or see the image he has built of himself.

It is also interesting to note how Echo desperately continues to long for Narcissus' attention, despite his disagreeable attitude and behavior. She continues to declare her love for him and wait for him in spite of everything. What's more, it's strange that she would be so smitten by someone only because of his looks. In the end she is reduced to a hardly discernible whisper. Such may be the fate of one who offers all of his or her loyalty and adulation to the narcissist.

Chapter 2

What Makes a Narcissist?

It was Freud who first introduced narcissism to the world of psychology in the early 1900s. Psychologists have come up with tests to determine whether a person may be considered a narcissist. Studies show that most narcissists tend to be male, although many are women. To keep things simple, the narcissist will oftentimes be referred to as "he" in this book. However, keep in mind that we could just as easily be referring to a female as a male..

9 Traits of the Narcissist

The following are 9 tell-tale traits which are dead giveaways when it comes to spotting a narcissist. Although this list is not conclusive, it's a great place to start.

Grandiosity

The narcissist expects to be recognized as superior despite a lack of evidence to back up his claims.

Preoccupation with power and success

They are obsessed with and have illusions of power, brilliance, beauty and ideal love.

Lack of empathy

They are unable or unwilling to recognize or identify with the feelings or needs of others.

Arrogant and domineering

They feel superior to others and wish to control and dominate.

Excessive need for admiration

They crave attention and resent it when others in the spotlight.

Exploitation of others

They have no qualms about taking advantage of others and sucking them dry. They only care about getting what they can from others.

Belief in being unique

They feel that they are special and that they can only be understood by or associate with others who are also as unique and special as they are.

Having a sense of entitlement

They have unreasonable expectations from others and believe that people owe them favors. They feel no gratitude for what others do for them.

Being envious of others

As they feel entitled, they are resentful when others have what they want. They also tend to assume that others are envious of them.

After reading these traits, familiar characters may come to mind like Lucy in *Charlie Brown,* Miranda Priestly (played by Meryl Streep) of *The Devil Wears Prada,* Tony Stark of *Ironman,* Scarlett O'Hara of *Gone with the Wind* and Dorian in *The Picture of Dorian Gray,* among many others.

Narcissist vs. NPD

Narcissistic personality disorder or NPD was recognized by The American Psychology Association in 1980. People who possess narcissistic traits do not necessarily have NPD. Narcissism can come in different degrees. A person who possesses at least five of the traits mentioned is said to have NPD.

Narcissists are easier to spot because of their flagrant obnoxious behavior. People with NPD, however, tend to be more devious and two-faced. They deceive people into believing them to be charming and outstanding models of society. They only show their true, diabolic selves to their "Echoes"- the people most devoted to them. Their narcissistic traits are deeply-woven into their being and they guard their image fastidiously. They will hide their true selves until they have gained your love and trust.

Amazingly, they may actually believe in the façade that they present to others. They are delusional about their capabilities and achievements. They think so highly of themselves that they consider criticism as a personal affront. They feel no remorse for mistreating others and have no true friends. They see nothing wrong in destroying the reputation of others as long as they gain from it.

The person with NPD sees himself as a god and everyone else is beneath him. He is always hungry for attention and needs continuous stimulation of his ego. If his needs are not met, he feels entitled to punishing the delinquent subject. He borders on being a sociopath. It is said that not all narcissists are sociopaths but all sociopaths are narcissists.

Causes of Narcissism

The real cause of NPD is still unknown but there some possible factors. The narcissist may have grown up under extreme styles of parenting (excessive praise or criticism); it could be something to do with genetics; he may have an over-sensitive personality; his parents or caregivers may have modeled manipulative behavior; he may have been abused in childhood; he may have extremely low self-esteem; or he may have had parents who used him as a source of their own self-esteem. Brain abnormality may also be a factor. New-found fame or wealth can bring about an acquired narcissism.

Overt and Covert Narcissism

As the name suggests, the overt narcissist is easy to identify. His narcissism is plain to see. He behaves grandiosely, is boastful, and demands special treatment. The overt narcissist feels slighted when he is criticized or when he feels unappreciated. He is convinced of his superiority and expects admiration for his real or perceived qualities. If his wishes are not met, he becomes aggressive or goes into a rage.

The covert narcissist, on the other hand, is sly in his dealings with people. He extracts the devotion he craves from people more cunningly than the overt narcissist. The covert narcissist may not publicly fly into a rage and may appear humble and kind; but he is just as or possibly more menacing and ruthless.

Both the overt and covert narcissists have deep feelings of insecurity. They both will resort to manipulative tactics to get affirmation or praise. The overt may use intimidation to do this while the covert will use more passive-aggressive methods. Both feel no guilt about taking from others or putting others down to get what they want. Remember that they are exploitative and will take what they want and never give in return. If ever they do give, it would most likely be in order to get something in return. There is no clear demarcation line between these two types of narcissists and their characteristics may overlap. A covert may also fly in a rage and overt may resort to passive aggressive maneuverings as well, for example. The covert narcissist, in general, is more difficult to detect than the overt narcissist.

On the rise

Is this generation a generation of narcissists? Is the proliferation of selfies and the popularity of cosmetic surgery proof of this? It is estimated that one to thirty-five percent of the population is narcissistic. It is still difficult to determine accurately because there may be a number of cases that have not yet been diagnosed. Many believe, however, that narcissism characterizes this generation as a whole.

When it's not a bad thing

Narcissistic traits are present in everyone and they are believed to be necessary for human development. Healthy narcissism is responsible for such positive qualities such as self-esteem, confidence, ambition, creativity and general well-being. It is a healthy self-love that enables a person to love others as well.

People who possess some narcissistic traits are viewed as having more exciting and likable personalities. Companies value the confidence, leadership and innovativeness of narcissists. As long as the person exhibits the positive aspects of narcissism realistically, it is considered healthy. Problems begin when the traits become excessive, imagined and pathological.

One major clue that the level of narcissism is no longer healthy is when failure of relationships exists.

Chapter 3

The Narcissist's Drug

The narcissist is a junkie who needs to get his fix all the time. This is what validates his existence or gives meaning to his life. To get his fix, the narcissist first creates his image or false self. This is a fictitious image that he has made up to present the kind of person that he dreams of being but knows he is not. He props up this façade as a kind of bait to bring in the reactions that he craves. The response to this image that he has set up is what feeds his ego. This is called the narcissistic supply, of which the narcissist can never get enough.

Narcissistic Supply

Narcissistic supply is what the narcissist needs to thrive in this world. He is like a vampire who needs not blood but a steady source of attention, admiration, approval, help and support. To him, life is meaningless without the narcissistic supply. In fact, he will still gratefully accept even negative attention. To the narcissist attention is appreciated, whether it be negative or positive. Unlike a normal person who also enjoys affirmation and approval in a moderate amount, the narcissist is never satisfied. He must have more because it is his drug. He craves this supply obsessively and will find ways to obtain it anywhere and anyway he can. He may obtain it from his spouse, girlfriend, friends, co-workers or even strangers. The source is not always a person. His career, talent, pet, or possessions may also fulfill his need for narcissistic supply.

Primary Narcissistic Supply

This refers to the general supply of attention that the narcissist obtains randomly. This supply may be public; such as fame, recognition, and even notoriety. It may also be something supplied privately; like a compliment or an insult. If the narcissist's craving were for water, then his primary supply would be the vast ocean.

Secondary Narcissistic Supply

This refers to the supply that the narcissist can count on to be there on a regular basis. Going back to the water analogy, if his primary supply is the vast ocean then his secondary supply would be the bottles of water he keeps in his refrigerator. The narcissist makes sure that he has a ready supply kept where he can avail of it whenever he wants it. He gets it from people or things that he comes in contact with on a regular basis- his coworkers, students, and most especially his spouse.

As the narcissist is very image conscious, the secondary supply is what he uses to perpetuate his false self. Most often, he wishes to make it appear that he is normal, successful, stable, influential and even a little mysterious.

Narcissist's Injury

It may be apparent by now that the narcissist's supply is what he uses to fill the emptiness that is so real to him. As long as he has his supply, he is fine. But what happens if the supply is cut off? Having to face the bottomless pit inside him will cause the narcissist to feel the way the drug abuser would if his fix were taken away from him- withdrawal symptoms. It will make him feel perplexed and agitated. It may even lead to an episode of psychosis. The narcissist cannot accept or admit to himself that he is in need.

Narcissistic injury is what he feels when his ego has been compromised. Still unable to accept that his elaborately-set up false image is imperfect, the narcissist's god complex takes over and he vows to exact revenge on whoever is responsible for withholding his supply. Delusionally, the narcissist believes himself to be injured.

Narcissist's Rage

The narcissist does not want to see himself as a victim. But the blocking of the flow of narcissistic supply makes him feel he has been slighted. Narcissist's rage is his reaction to the blocking of his precious supply. His reaction would be to get back or lash out at the culprit and to promptly get back to re-establishing a steady flow of his narcissistic supply. His rage can range from mild to physically violent. It may be passive-aggressive, pernicious or downright violent. In the eyes of the narcissist, his outburst of rage is completely warranted because he has been assaulted. But, to the normal person, his rage is an unwarranted reaction to a series of neutral events.

Chapter 4

Spotting the Narcissist

Not everyone who brags or is vain is a narcissist. Each one of us has some of the traits mentioned in the previous chapter but that doesn't automatically make us all narcissists. It is important to be able to spot the narcissist in your life because he can leave you emotionally or even physically battered. The narcissist will exploit or hurt others without any feelings of remorse. His own personal gain is all that matters to him.

It is when the narcissist believes (it's just what he thinks) he is not receiving the esteem, affection or adoration he craves, that he will bear his fangs or show his evil self. Often, the one who is most devoted to him will be the one to suffer. A narcissist might respond to difficult times with mood swings, having affairs, using drugs, resorting to alcohol, lashing out verbally or physically, or exhibiting a variety of inappropriate and hurtful behaviors.

If there is something in your relationship that makes you feel uncomfortable, bothered or ashamed and you hesitate to tell even those closest to you, you may be in a relationship with a narcissist. Ordinary boastfulness may annoy you somewhat, but the narcissist will cause more than normal anguish or emotional stress.

Narcissists, the covert narcissist in particular, can be good at hiding their true selves. But, with awareness, you can spot him in different situations and spare yourself a lot of suffering. The narcissistic traits are easy to recognize in the overt narcissist; you need to be more observant and alert with the covert narcissist.

Dating the Narcissist

He lavishes you with attention and praise.

It may thrill you that he seems truly enamored with you. He is never out of compliments and he bombards you with presents, text messages, flowers, phone calls and Facebook likes. Everything seems too much and too soon, and it may well be. Be wary because this is a common technique used by narcissists and scammers to lure you to their web (see "love bombing" in Chapter 5).

He's smooth and charming.

His predatory instincts and experience make him a master at wooing his prey. He will play Prince Charming in order to trap you.

He promises the moon.

The narcissist likes to make grandiose promises, especially in the presence of witnesses to show what a great guy he is. Give it time and see if he follows through with his promises because he often forgets or has no intention of fulfilling them in the first place.

He puts down his ex.

He describes her as a scheming gold-digger and criticizes all the others he's had a relationship with. And then he tells you that you are different in hopes to win your affection. The narcissist seldom takes blame or responsibility for his own mistakes; it is always someone else's fault. He may also blame his father, his boss, his coworker and everyone else. He will try to win your sympathy by playing the victim.

He expresses either intense love or intense hate for his mom.

The primary caregiver of the narcissist may most likely be one as well. The child usually has a love-hate and toxic relationship with the narcissistic parent.

He name-drops.

To try to impress you without seeming boastful, he casually mentions names of famous people he knows. He might also mention his achievements, places his been to or property that he owns. He is building himself up to make you fall for him more easily.

He's rude to the waiter.

The narcissist's feelings of entitlement and lack of empathy may come out with people he doesn't feel obliged to impress. He may try to wheedle or coerce to get a table without a reservation or put the waiter (or taxi driver, receptionist, valet, etc.) to shame for some insignificant offense.

He's too much in charge.

Women are usually impressed by men who are good decision makers and who know about ordering food or wine on dates. But the narcissist will not consider your own needs and will fail to even ask about what you want.

He's in a hurry.

He rushes you into sex or a relationship; he may even offer marriage right away. Does he start talking about having children and plans for your future as a couple too early in the relationship? The narcissist is impatient because he can't pretend for too long.

It is best to leave early on in the relationship. Do not think that you can change the narcissist. His issues are too deeply rooted for him to change. Spare yourself the heartache and abuse and leave while you can.

The Narcissistic Friend

He seems very charming and friendly at first.

The narcissist will use his charm to befriend someone who has something he wants. He will seem very nice at the beginning but will change after he's gotten what he wants.

He is surrounded by a posse.

The narcissist has no real friends, only people he needs to get what he wants. His so-called friends are mere acquaintances who come and go in his life. He soon leaves them when they no longer supply what he needs and goes on to charm new

"friends."

It's not easy to open up to him about your secrets or fears.

If you try opening up to him, he will mock you, put you down or show no sympathy whatsoever. Even though you were there for him when he was down, he is unable to give back when you need support.

He expects you to agree with him on everything.

He cannot accept anyone who disagrees with him and may respond by shaming you or giving you the cold shoulder.

You will always be just the side kick.

The narcissist will never let you share the spotlight. Everything will be about him. He will dominate your conversations and stir all attention towards himself.

You will feel something off about your friendship.

You may be unable to pinpoint what it is, but encounters with the narcissist will make you feel bothered, used or violated. That's because you friendship is based on his manipulation of you so that his own needs are met.

The narcissist is not able to be a true friend and you cannot change him. Some people have their reasons for maintaining their ties with the narcissist. To survive, you have to set boundaries to avoid being abused. You may refer to chapter 5 for ways to deal with the narcissist.

In the Family

The Narcissistic Parent

It is particularly difficult for children of a narcissistic parent because they usually do not know what is wrong until they're older and are trying to deal with their own issues. Many only realize that their parents are narcissists when they are already grown up and they are struggling to undo the damage done to them. To the outside world, the narcissistic parents seem like the perfect parents because this is the image they project. Sadly, the children suffer in secret.

They use their children to build up their own image.

As with all narcissists, narcissistic parents have a very low self esteem and try to fulfill their unrealized dreams through their children. They place undue pressure on their children to be perfect and they fear being criticized by others because of their children's imperfections. The children also consequently lose their sense of identity and are disconnected from their own needs and desires because their parents had been living vicariously through them all their lives.

They are stingy with their children but not with themselves.

The will shame their children for voicing their needs. The children eventually grow to be easy prey because they have learned to give in to the narcissist. They grow up feeling they do not deserve things they are actually entitled to.

They pit their children against each other.

This is the narcissistic parent's way to ensure complete loyalty from their children. They play favorites and pit them against each other as a form of manipulation so that their own needs are met. The parents hate the child that reflects their own inadequacies and smother the one they think possesses their good qualities. The siblings grow up not resentful of each other.

They fail to see their children as separate individuals.

Because they see their children as only extensions of themselves, they disregard boundaries and intrude into their children's privacy, reading their letters or emails, dictating what the children should wear, interfering with their personal lives and treating them with total disrespect.

They force their children to assume responsibilities or roles inappropriate to their age.

The parents play the pity party with their children, forcing the children to act more like the spouse or parent than the child. The narcissistic parent doesn't care how much this may be damaging to the child, as long as their own needs are met.

They never say sorry.

They will never own up to their mistakes, never apologize to their children. It will always be somebody else's fault, never their own. They will not hesitate to lie or destroy their own children's reputation to save their own. They will make it appear that their children are evil and ungrateful despite their being the perfect parents.

It is important for children of narcissistic parents to seek help from a professional. They must also understand what made their parents narcissists and they must try to build bridges with their siblings. If the narcissistic parent is abusive, it would be best for the children to seek help and move to a safe place.

The Narcissistic Spouse

Sees you as an ever-flowing spring of narcissistic supply.

You should be able to anticipate his needs before he asks. You are expected to supply support and adoration on-call. You will have to give until you run dry while the narcissist will never give anything in return. If he has the impression that your supply has stopped, expect narcissistic rage.

Is unreasonably jealous.

As you are their constant supply of their fix, they do not want anything to get in the way of that supply. Don't be surprised if they are jealous of everything and everyone – even your brother, his sister, your children, his father or the family pet.

Projects all his inadequacies or unacceptable onto you.

The narcissist will call you needy and ungrateful. He will accuse you of being insatiable and unreasonable. But he is the only person who says so. He may accuse you of being lazy, a liar, a flirt or a cheater; all of which reflect his own doings. Of course, in the narcissist's own eyes, he can do no wrong.

Antagonizes you.

He will do this because he wants to provoke you to leave. To the narcissist, this is proof of what he had always suspected (actually, feared) that you would leave him. He can also use it against you by making it appear that he is the victim.

He may also be the one to threaten to leave, especially if he knows you will beg him to stay.

'

Gives you the silent treatment.

He will do this with no explanations, just to torture you. It is a classic passive-aggressive method of abuse. It is his way of putting you down, without using words, and of assuming control. Later, he will treat you as though nothing happened and expect you to welcome him back without protest.

Is a flirt and has affairs.

It is because of his constant and insatiable need for affirmation. He cannot resist the thrill of winning a new lover. Because if his distorted view of himself, he is convinced that even innocently friendly women are flirting with him.

Is addicted to porn.

Many narcissists have a tendency to be addicted to porn as this is another available narcissistic supply. Also, online affairs can be a convenient way for them to manipulate people.

Abuses you.

He may abuse you emotionally, sexually, psychologically or physically. The purpose of this abuse is to dominate and ensure that you never stop providing narcissistic supply. The reality is that the narcissist is not in love with you, he has always only been after your supply.

Says sorry and expects things to go back to normal.

This is another abusive tactic. He may or may not sound sincere in showing remorse, but what is strange is his expectation that things can get back to normal instantaneously. But he may have programmed you in such a way that you will immediately accept him without question.

The narcissist is unlikely to change, although it is possible. Anyone who has a narcissistic spouse should see a professional and decide whether it would be wise to stay in the relationship or not. Leaving is usually the better option.

The Narcissistic Teen

Teenagers typically go through a phase of self-obsession but they eventually grow out it. Although narcissism can be diagnosed as early as the age of eighteen, it will take a trained professional to do so and after observation over a certain period of time. Narcissistic teenagers exhibit the same traits as the adult narcissist, but remember that what you may see as narcissistic behavior may simply be a stage in their development. Here are some of the more serious signs of narcissism in teenagers.

They have a larger than life image of themselves.

They seem to see themselves as superior, more talented, or better-looking than they really are and they propagate this image in social media or by boasting and self-praise. They become angry and resentful, even aggressive, when this image of themselves is questioned.

They think they can get away with hurting others.

They are completely lacking in empathy and believe the world owes them so they can do anything they like even if it will be morally, emotionally or physically damaging to another person.

They fail repeatedly in their interpersonal relationships.

They can't seem to get along with anyone. They always want to dominate others. It is difficult for them to establish healthy relationships. They are always in trouble at school or at work.

They show signs of depression.

Watch for prolonged sadness accompanied by lethargy, irritability, anger, tearfulness, withdrawal from family and friends, and irregular eating and sleeping habits.

They are suicidal.

The narcissistic teen will need to undergo therapy and learn to have a healthy sense of self-worth and to learn to establish healthy relationships. Medication may be needed for depression and anxiety. Family support will be very to helpful at this stage. Yoga, massage therapy and other holistic approaches to healing can also be helpful. Self-medication is not advised.

At Work

The Narcissistic Boss or Co-worker

Is very charismatic.

He has exceptional charm and energy. People are attracted to him and see him as a kind and competent person. Unfortunately, this charm deceptively covers up the narcissist's lack of feelings or empathy.

Praises inordinately.

He thinks that he can manipulate you with flattery but it's easy to sense his insincerity.

Will put you down.

To shame others makes the narcissist feel more powerful. He also has no empathy and doesn't care how shaming you in public may affect you.

Has favorites.

He has a hand-picked select group of people who he is dependent on for narcissistic supply. These people may or may not be good at their job; the important thing is they help feed his ego.

Does not accept criticism.

The narcissistic boss or co-worker does not want anyone to criticize or question his ideas. He may put you to shame in front of everyone or react aggressively when contradicted.

Feels above-the-law.

Breaking rules is something he does nonchalantly and against everyone's advice. It's no big deal to him.

Takes credit for others' work.

They have no conscience and taking credit for something they did not do is simply routine to them.

Makes false promises.

The promise is simply done to manipulate you and, if done in front of others, to impress. If you ask about it, he will either deny it or make even more false promises to keep you hoping.

Likes to flirt, bordering on sexual harassment.

Because he feels above the law and has no boundaries, being in a position of power, he may use this to make advances or harass you sexually. This is another tool he uses to manipulate.

Will fire or demote you.

After benefiting from your hard work, skills and talent, he will drop you like a hot potato because you are no longer useful to him.

The Narcissist On Facebook

Facebook is the narcissist's haven because it is where he gets a steady narcissistic supply. The narcissist will maximize the benefits by deliberately setting up his Facebook posts and comments to attract as many likes and reactions as possible.

Regularly and repeatedly posts well thought-out selfies.

He has taken pains to position the camera and to pose in such a way as to show off his best features to gain likes and praises (or even insults) from everyone. The narcissist wants to show off his perceived superiority in terms of looks or status and will makes numerous selfies in a day.

Consistently posts selfies to brag.

He wants to show off the new expensive signature item he just bought, the exclusive resort he just went to for a vacation, his new car, etc. Normal people post photos to update friends and family or to share their experiences but the narcissist's posts clearly say "Look at how good-looking/sexy/jet-setting/ rich/cool/ successful I am" every time.

Does not hesitate to ask for compliments.

The narcissist is not ashamed to ask for likes and compliments outright. After all, this is the reason he's on FB.

Uses FB to influence people to gang up on, insult or bully another person.

He does not care how his posts or comments may destroy another person's life and reputation, as long as he succeeds in posting something that will attract a lot of attention.

Spends more time on FB than doing his job or going about normal activities.

He is so addicted to the narcissistic supply on FB that he neglects responsibilities at school or work, neglects to exercise, eat, sleep or meet up with people.

By now you may have spotted narcissists in your midst and want to know what to do next. This is what we'll discuss in the next chapter.

Chapter 5

Dealing with the Narcissist

After reading the previous chapters, it may now be clear to you that you are or a person you know is dealing with a narcissist. What's the next step? For one, being informed is the first step to breaking away and stopping the narcissist from destroying your life.

How do I know if I'm being abused by a narcissist?

This may sound like a stupid question. Many people looking on the outside can't understand why the abused person finds it so hard to leave the abuser. It is not as simple as it looks. Abuse is not always physical and can be very subtle and difficult to detect. The victim needs to snap out of the spell that the narcissist has cast to realize this. Even when the victim is aware, it is still difficult to leave. Here are some of signs that you are being abused by the narcissist:

- You've lost your self confidence and assertiveness. You always feel unsure about yourself and you find it difficult to express your opinions.

- You no longer are or are hardly in contact with you family and friends. You feel isolated from others. I once met a victim of abuse who told me she felt that, if she died, no one would come to her funeral.

- Friends and family express concern regarding you situation and about how you are being treated.

- You feel sad or depressed, anxious and uneasy and you no longer enjoy the things that you used to.

- After a having an argument or even just a conversation with the narcissist, you feel that everything you said is wrong or stupid.

- You notice that the narcissist is engaging, kind and charming in front of other people but is critical, condescending and avoidant when he is with you.

- You no longer care about your looks or your health. Personal grooming seems to take so much effort.

- If you have children, you notice that they are in distress as well.

- You are the one giving and doing everything to keep the relationship together. The narcissist expects this from you and does nothing to help.

- You have a sense of doing all the giving but receiving no love in return.

- You can't understand why the narcissist is always blaming you for, or accusing you of, things you never even would have thought of doing.

How did you get yourself into a relationship

with a narcissist?

There are some traits that may cause us to fall into the narcissist's trap.

Empathy

The narcissist is a wounded, hurting and empty. The empath's sensitivity and love are just what the narcissist is looking for. But the empath mistakenly assumes he or she can fix the narcissist. The narcissist cannot be fixed. His intention is to break the empath in order to be in control. The narcissist has a god complex, so when he meets someone who is willing to make sacrifices for a relationship, it is just too irresistible.

Kindness

You are eager to please and you readily dish out praises. When someone is hurt, you are quick to ease the pain. The narcissist recognizes the spring of narcissistic supply that you are and he wants that. Again, it's not because he loves you (although it may fit his twisted definition of love), it's because he wants that supply.

Vulnerability

Even without the traits that the narcissist finds appealing, if you are willing to let the narcissist into your life, he will. You may be a die-hard romantic or are afraid to be alone. He may have fooled you into thinking he'd help you financially. Whatever you vulnerability is, the narcissist took advantage of it. That is the nature of the narcissist.

Credulity

Being kind and well-intentioned, you had no idea that the narcissist exists. You believed in narcissist's tactics of deception. You used to think that everyone is as nice as you are and the narcissist took advantage of that.

The Narcissist's Mind Games

It's important to go back to how you had been deceived in order to avoid falling into the same trap.

Love bombing

This is the usual first step in dating. He will drop "bombs" of notes, messages throughout the day, calls, presents, flowers, chocolates; anything to make you drop your defenses and make you believe he truly loves you. You may sense some insincerity in his love bombing but you brush it aside and let yourself go with the flow. You begin to fall for all the attention and become an easy target for his ultimate goal to control and manipulate you.

Listening

You marvel at what a good listener he is. He appears to be genuinely interested in you because he asks questions and seems to be making mental notes as you speak. What he is doing is gathering information and tracking vulnerabilities. He is indeed taking mental notes in order to know how to manipulate you. Being a good listener is normally a positive trait. But, if he seems to be overly inquisitive at once and, if he inundates you with too many personal questions, listen to the warning bells.

Mirroring

He will try to convince you that you are very similar to each other by always to pointing out how similar you are. The important thing to the narcissist is to trap you. So he will agree with everything you say, laugh at all your jokes, claim to like the same food, book, movies- anything to hook you.

Silent treatment

This is another punishment used for a perceived offense. The narcissist will do this for different periods of time without explanation to torture you. It is a passive aggressive form of abuse. It gives him control over you and is particularly distressing because you are suffering but the reason is not tangible.

Pity

He will make you feel that he has suffered so much from his cheating wife, abusive parent, unscrupulous boss, crazy ex, and so on and so forth. He wants to appeal to your sense of pity and stimulate you nurturing instincts. Later in the relationship, if you threaten to leave, he may tell you he's dying of some terminal illness like cancer.

Triangulation

He creates a triangle with you and another person – a parent, coworker, mistress or child, and pits the two of you against each other. This puts him off the hook and successfully makes you feel insecure about your relationship and desperate to hold on. He dusts his hands off as he watches the two of you in conflict.

Gas lighting

The technique by which the narcissist deviously makes you doubt you perception of things as well as your sanity. He will convince you that you saw wrong, you heard wrong, you misunderstood, it didn't happen that way, and so on until you doubt yourself and believe everything he tells you.

Projection

He will project all his misdeeds or feelings on you as if they were yours. He will call you a cheater because he is secretly cheating on you. He will say you are a liar because he kept so many truths from you. This leaves you bewildered, defensive and broken.

Hoovering

Taken from the vacuum cleaner brand, this is the narcissist's attempt to suck you back to him. He will pretend to have changed, send you messages, ask about the kids, appear meek, promise to see a therapist, etc. His ultimate goal is get back his supply. He will try his best to convince you that things will change, if you'd just come back.

Blaming and guilt

He will pass the blame on you to make you feel guilty. He will make it appear that everything is your fault, you brought it all on yourself. You refused to have sex, you were such a nagger, you gained weight, you complained too much, you neglected him, you put your career first and so on. He will convince you that he became bad because of you, you made him do it. He may convince you that he's telling the truth and get you to give him his supply all over again.

Dealing with the Narcissist

Now that you've realized that there is a narcissist in your life, what should you do?

Take a step back and analyze the situation.

Determine how bad the situation is. Try to understand the narcissist's background and his degree of his narcissism. Note or recall what drives him to narcissistic rage. Recall how he tries to punish you. Be aware of the tactics that he uses. Do all these objectively. Being carried away by emotions, shouting or crying will only feed the narcissist. The narcissist has already painstakingly set up a strong image or reputation and you might not come across as credible when you tell others, so you have to do your homework.

Accept that the narcissist will not change.

Hoping that you will be able to knock some sense into the narcissist or that you could explain and things to enlighten him will not work. As far as the narcissist is concerned, he has done no wrong.

Seek help.

Find people – friends, counselors, religious leaders, or parents- any one you can confide in and who can give advice and emotional support. They can also give feedback from a neutral viewpoint.

Set boundaries.

Write down which boundaries the narcissist cannot trespass and a consequence if they do. Writing things down before talking to the narcissist will help you speak without sounding emotional.

Be realistic.

Know the narcissist's limitations and work within those limits. It will only be emotionally draining and a waste of time to expect more from the narcissist than he is capable. Do not expect him to learn to care because he can't.

Remember that your value as a person does not depend on the narcissist.

Don't punish yourself for getting into a relationship with him. Instead, focus on rebuilding your self-esteem, meeting your own needs and pursuing your interests.

Speak to them in a way that will make them aware of how they will benefit.

Instead of voicing you needs, pleading, crying or yelling; learn to rephrase your statements by emphasizing what the narcissist will gain from it. You have learn to appeal to their selfishness. This is a good way to survive in situations when you cannot leave.

Bring up your ideas to the narcissistic boss when there are witnesses.

By having others around to hear your idea, he will find it difficult to claim credit for it.

Find proof of or document any kind of abuse.

Make use of technology- CCTV or video recordings, for example- to document instances of abuse. Find witnesses to back you up.

Do not fall for the narcissist's tactics again.

Refresh yourself on his tactics and be on your guard against falling for them again. The narcissist may try to use pity, projection or hoovering. This time, be wiser. It may take practice, as you may have become used to being the "Echo" or codependent. Being aware will help you to resist.

Leave.

The best way to deal with the narcissist is not to. For the sake of you emotional and physical well-being, not to mention your sanity, it would be best to leave. If you do leave, expect various tactics from the narcissist to either make your life miserable or to get you (actually his supply) back. You will also undergo a period of distress, akin to mourning when you leave. Seek help and support to get through this stage. Do not be hard on yourself for having allowed yourself to be deceived by the narcissist. Your experience will make you stronger, wiser and, in time, ready for a healthy relationship. In the meantime, focus on your own interests and rebuilding your self-esteem.

Chapter 6

Quotes To Help You Better Understand The Narcissist

"It is not love that should be depicted as blind, but self-love."

—Voltaire

"To love oneself is the beginning of a lifelong romance."

—Oscar Wilde

"Narcissism falls along the axis of what psychologists call personality disorders, one of a group that includes antisocial, dependent, histrionic, avoidant and borderline personalities. But by most measures, narcissism is one of the worst, if only because the narcissists themselves are so clueless."

—Jeffrey Kluger

"I think a lot of self-importance is a product of fear. And fear, living in sort of an un-self-examined fear-based life, tends to lead to narcissism and self-importance."

—Moby

"Since [narcissists] deep down feel themselves to be faultless, it is inevitable that when they are in conflict with the world they will invariably perceive the conflict as the world's fault."

—M. Scott Peck

"I love narcissists—even more than they love themselves. You don't have to buoy them up. They are their own razzle-dazzle show and you are the blessed, favored with a front-row seat."

—Patricia Marx

"The narcissist devours people, consumes their output, and casts the empty, writhing shells aside."

—Sam Vaknin

"If people are really narcissistic or have a need to be

seen as more than they really are, or to be admired

as having it all together, then they cannot be

followed and trusted by others."

—Henry Cloud

"Whether with a narcissist a week, a month, a year, a

decade, or a half of a century, one thing is for sure...

one day you will wake up to the revelation that it

was all just a figment of your imagination."

—Tigress Luv

"The most uninteresting thing in the world is watching narcissists fuck each other."

—Jarett Kobek

"He that falls in love with himself will have no rivals."

—Benjamin Franklin

"Narcissistic people are always struggling with the fact that the rest of the world doesn't revolve around them."

—Unknown

"Though they are quick to put others down, unhealthy narcissists view themselves in absolutely positive terms."

—Daniel Goleman

"There's a reason narcissists don't learn from mistakes and that's because they never get past the first step which is admitting that they made one."

—Jeffrey Kluger

"Some narcissistic people end up believing their own lies."

—Unknown

"Out of all the addictions in the world, attention is slowly but surely becoming one of the most dangerous."

—Saahil Prem

"Relationships with narcissists are held in place by hope of a 'someday better,' with little evidence to support it will ever arrive."

—Ramani Durvasula

"This Narcissus of ours

Can't see his face in the mirror

Because he has become the mirror."

—Antonio Machado

"I bet it gets pretty lonely with only your ego for

company."

—Alexandra Bracken

"How starved you must have been that my heart

became a meal for your ego."

—Amanda Torroni

"Self-love forever creeps out, like a snake, to sting

anything which happens...to stumble upon it."

—George Gordon Noel Byron

"A sociopath is one who sees others as impersonal objects to be manipulated to fulfill their own narcissistic needs without any regard for the hurtful consequences of their selfish actions."

—R. Alan Woods

"I think writers are the most narcissistic people. Well, I mustn't say this, I like many of them, a great many of my friends are writers."

—Sylvia Plath

"A narcissist paints a picture of themselves as being the victim or innocent in all aspects. They will be offended by the truth. But what is done in the dark will come to light. Time has a way of showing people's true colors."

—Karla Grimes

"The sadistic narcissist perceives himself as Godlike, ruthless and devoid of scruples, capricious and unfathomable, emotionless and non-sexual, omniscient, omnipotent and omnipresent, a plague, a devastation, an inescapable verdict."

—Sam Vaknin

"Love doesn't die a natural death. Love has to be killed, either by neglect or narcissism."

—Frank Salvato

"It is especially painful when narcissists suffer memory loss because they are losing parts of the person they love most."

—David Brooks

"Half the harm that is done in this world is due to people who want to feel important. They don't mean to do harm, but the harm (that they cause) does not interest them. Or they do not see it, or they justify it because they are absorbed in the endless struggle to think well of themselves."

—T. S. Eliot

"Narcissists have poor self-esteem, but they are typically very successful. They feel entitled; they're self-important; they crave admiration and lack empathy. They are also exploitative and envious. The malignant types never forget a slight. They may kill you ten years later for cutting them off in traffic. But they act perfectly normal while plotting their revenge."

—Janet M. Tavakoli

"Withhold admiration from a narcissist and be disliked. Give it and be treated with indifference."

—Mason Cooley

"Hate is the complement of fear and narcissists like being feared. It imbues them with an intoxicating sensation of omnipotence."

—Sam Vaknin

"I wonder if the course of narcissism through the ages would have been any different had Narcissus first peered into a cesspool. He probably did."

—Frank O'Hara

"Narcissistic personality disorder is named for Narcissus, from Greek mythology, who fell in love with his own reflection. Freud used the term to describe persons who were self-absorbed, and psychoanalysts have focused on the narcissist's need to bolster his or her self-esteem through grandiose fantasy, exaggerated ambition, exhibitionism, and feelings of entitlement."

—Donald W. Black

"A man who loves others based solely on how they make him feel, or what they do for him, is really not loving others at all—but loving only himself."

—Criss Jami

"The 'Selfie Stick' has to top the list for what best defines narcissism in society today."

—Alex Morritt

"The silent killer of all great men and women of achievement—particularly men, I don't know why, maybe it's the testosterone—I think it's narcissism. Even more than hubris. And for women, too. Narcissism is the killer."

—James Woods

"I am a recovering narcissist. I thought narcissism was about self-love till someone told me there is a flip side to it. It is actually drearier than self-love; it is unrequited self-love."

—Emily Levine

"Narcissus weeps to find that his image does not return his love."

—Mason Cooley

"The main condition for the achievement of love is the overcoming of one's narcissism."

—Erich Fromm

"Narcissists commonly cut people off and out of their lives due to their shallow emotional style of seeing others as either good or bad."

—Karyl McBride

"Narcissistic love is riding on the rollercoaster of disaster filled with a heart full of tears."

—Sheree Griffin

"There was nothing more unattractive than narcissism, she thought: nothing could transform beauty into a cloying, unattractive quality than that self-conscious appreciation of self."

—Alexander McCall Smith

"The paradox is that no love can prove so intense as the love of two narcissists for each other."

—Norman Mailer

"I have a very simple question to people...who seem to suffer from excessive narcissism: Please name three other persons who are smarter and more capable than you, in the field you work in. (In most cases they are utterly unable to answer that question honestly.)"

—Ingo Molnar

"A narcissist can't be faithful. This is because—to a narcissist—'you' don't exist except as a mirror. When he looks at you, all he sees is his own reflection. Distort this reflection and he will go find another mirror. It's as simple, or as complicated, as that."

—Tigress Luv

"Imagining that you are deep and complex, but others are simple, is one of the primary signs of malignant selfishness."

—Stefan Molyneux

"If anybody studying psychology wants a concrete example of what a narcissist looks like, I advise them to consider any man who cheats on his wife. These guys are the textbook me-firsters, the ones who think the rules don't apply to them, the ones who tell themselves as long as she doesn't know, there's no harm done. No woman needs to sleep with these guys. There are so many single self-absorbed narcissists who will fuck you poorly."

—Julie Klausner

"The only crime is pride."

—Sophocles

"The greater our own level of narcissism, the more

we detest it in others."

—Steve Maraboli

"When I look at narcissism through the vulnerability lens, I see the shame-based fear of being ordinary. I see the fear of never feeling extraordinary enough to be noticed, to be lovable, to belong, or to cultivate a sense of purpose."

—Brené Brown

<u>Conclusion</u>

I hope this book has given you a more thorough insight into understanding and dealing with the issue narcissism and narcissistic behavior.

Although it can be difficult, coping with these kinds of people is possible. And don't forget, if you can't change your situation you always have the power to leave it!

Don't forget to scroll down for your FREE GIFTS and for more info on my other books!

A message from the author,

Jane Aniston

To show my appreciation for your support, Id like to offer you a couple of exclusive free gifts:

FREE BONUS!

As a free bonus, I've included a preview of onc of my other best-selling books directly after this section. Enjoy!

ALSO...

Be sure to check out my other books. Scroll to the back of this book for a list of other books written by me, along with download links.

Finally, if you enjoyed this book, **please** take the time to post a review on Amazon. It will only take a couple of minutes and I'd be extremely grateful for your support.

Thank you again for your support.

Jane Aniston

FREE BONUS!: Preview Of

"Difficult People -

Understanding & Dealing

With Difficult People"

If you enjoyed this book, I have a little bonus for you;

a preview of one of my other books, "Difficult People -

Understanding & Dealing With Difficult People".

Enjoy!

Introduction

Human beings are the most difficult people,

in the world. I don't get them.

~ Unknown

We've all run into difficult people in our lives. These people may be your boss, girlfriend, parent, roommate, co-worker, teacher, landlord, next-door neighbor, uncle, sister, son, daughter or, perhaps worst of all, the person you've vowed to spend the rest of your life with!

Ideally, relationships should be rich, fertile media which allow for enjoyable interactions as well as personal growth. A healthy relationship provides such positive benefits as affirmation, encouragement, and enlightenment. Sometimes, just a short chat with a good friend is enough to make you feel that the world is beautiful indeed. After dealing with a likable, affirming, person who is not "difficult", we are often left feeling whole, inspired, happy and confident.

The difficult person, on the other hand, is an emotional vampire who sucks up all your energy. Difficult people can leave you exhausted, disoriented, shattered, and insecure.

With the difficult person, everything you thought was good and right becomes a lie. You begin to question yourself. After even a short conversation with a difficult person, you may find yourself feeling a whole host of negative emotions. Spend too much time around them and you may eventually find yourself losing faith in yourself and in humanity. Difficult people beat you up emotionally, mentally and spiritually.

Unfortunately, it isn't always possible to simply walk away from people who make your life miserable; you can't always just suck it up and go on your way. However, it is said that change is the beginning of understanding, and this book will help you understand difficult people and give you tips on how to handle them. You'll see that you don't always have to end up emotionally black-and-blue, and that there are ways to deal with difficult people.

Chapter 1

Different Strokes for Different Difficult

Folks

"I don't like that man. I must get to know him

better."

— Abraham Lincoln

Abraham Lincoln got it right when he said that. We've got to know the difficult person better. Know what makes that person tick and know how to duck when he throws his arrows at you. And if you get to know him really well, you may even convince him to tuck his arrows back into his quiver.

So let's get to know who these "stress carriers", these "toxic people" are. Some are easy to spot and almost instantly repulsive. Not all difficult people are obvious, though. Some of them can be charming and very likable, easily breaking down your defenses, and you can find yourself bruised and broken without realizing what hit you.

In this chapter we'll take a look at these shady characters who can make our lives difficult, and then , in the succeeding chapters, we'll pin point just how to deal with them.

Arrogant Arthur and Haughty Hannah

Arrogant Arthur and Haughty Hannah always assume that things should go their way. There are no buts or ifs with them. The only best and right way is theirs. Arrogant Arthur is selfish, demanding and insensitive - an all-around @#*%. Haughty Hannah has no qualms about hurting yours or anyone else's feelings because she is always right and there's nothing you can do about it. They can be exciting to be with, as they're always on fire and on the go; but as far as they're concerned, you're so lucky to be with them because they're so unique and special. They see themselves as superior; so they deserve all that is good and beautiful. Don't expect them to be around when you really need them.though They don't have time for your little dramas or sob stories. They only need you when they can get something from you. There's no give and take with them, all they do take, take, take.

Tyra Tyrant and Desmond Despot

Tyra Tyrant and Desmond Despot are a bit like Arrogant Arthur and Haughty Hannah, maybe twin siblings. They think very highly of themselves so they are very demanding and opinionated. They want to dominate and force their way on everyone. But they believe they're actually doing the world a favor because they've got the best ideas on the planet. Don't you ever, ever criticize them because, in their eyes, it is simply inconceivable for them to be wrong. If you question or criticize them, prepare for a barrage of insults, intimidating tactics, or even violence. Tyra Tyrant and Desmond Despot are the ultimate bullies.

Thea Theatric and Hiro Histrionic

You'll never miss these two when they walk into a room. Everything about them is about drama and attention-getting. They aren't comfortable when no one notices them. They can be extraordinarily good-looking and flirtatious. They want you to notice them and see how beautiful, smart and wonderful they are. If you don't, they will force you to notice them through exaggerated movements and expressions. When you see them, it feels like they're always performing before an audience. They dress flamboyantly and seductively. Though seemingly sociably competent, they also come off as shallow and manipulative. Sometimes, they resort to inappropriate behavior just to get the attention they crave.

Oscar Obsessive and Chloe Compulsive

These two are identical twins, maybe even conjoined. They take themselves seriously and, well, they don't think you're funny. They don't think anything's funny, for that matter. They are rigid, dogmatic and authoritative. They give exceptional attention to detail and they know exactly how everything should be done. Any deviation from their way will drive them nuts. They are highly knowledgeable and well-informed about a wide range of topics and they can be valuable at work because of their competence and meticulousness. They are organized and exact in everything they do. At times they have little rituals that they follow just to make sure everything is just perfect. An encounter with them could make you feel inferior and weak.

Nick Nice and Abby Agreeable

They're such delightful people, these two. They're friendly and easygoing. You see them in cliques or with a wide social circle. It's easy to feel at ease with them. No pressure or feeling of being judged. You seldom get any resistance from these people, it's as if they can't say 'no.' However, herein lies the problem; they can never say no! Nick Nice and Abby Agreeable are such people-pleasers that they can't say no even when they should. They procrastinate and neglect obligations. They fail to follow through with their promises because they tend to bite off more than they can chew.

Fiona Faultfinder and Cris Critic

Fiona Faultfinder and Cris Critic have made it their job to criticize everything and everyone. They do it 24/7. Talk about seeing the speck of dirt on a white sheet of paper. But don't take it personally; it's for your own good, really. In the guise of being concerned or giving friendly advice, these two will dish out every flaw they 'see' in you. They may delve into areas where they have no business, but it is still really to help you.

They believe they are the eyes that see what you can't see. Unfortunately, while they are generous with criticism, you will hardly hear an uplifting word from them. Another thing that they gripe about is that you never thank them for pointing out all that's wrong with you. After being with them, you'll feel guilty, inadequate and quite ashamed of yourself.

Gloria Gloom and Perry Pessimist

You might remember a character in *Gilligan's Island* who kept saying "We'll never make it." Same with *Eeyore* in Winnie the Pooh. Such dismal characters. Gloria Gloom and Perry Pessimist are always the first to point out what could go wrong. While others see a light around the bend, they see a problem at every corner. Don't take them on a boat ride because they're certain the boat will sink; don't try out the new Mexican restaurant, the food is sure to taste horrible. Nothing will turn out right. They're not very adventurous and will avoid taking risks. They lend an atmosphere of heavy doom and gloom to any setting.

Mary Martyr and Ned Needy

If anything can go wrong, it will go wrong for these two. Their lives are an endless series of unfortunate incidents. Mary Martyr and Ned Needy are helpless, clingy, and dependent. They send signals that they need to be rescued and they never seem to learn from their mistakes. It's no wonder you'll most likely find them in abusive relationships. Be careful though, their helplessness is also their way of manipulating other people.

Now that you've been introduced to the kinds of difficult people you might encounter (or most likely HAVE encountered) in your life, it should be easier for you to spot them and not be caught by surprise.

Check out the rest of "Difficult People - Understanding & Dealing With Difficult People" on Amazon.

Check Out My Other Books!

Understanding Anxiety - *Why You're Suffering From Anxiety & How You Can Start Breaking Free!*

Overcoming Anxiety -*Practical Approaches You Can Use To Manage Fear & Anxiety In The Moment & Long Term*

Depression - Practical & Natural Approaches You Can Use To Cure Depression In The Moment & Long Term

Cognitive Behavioral Therapy - A Practical Guide To C.B.T. For Overcoming Anxiety, Depression, Addictions & Other Psychological Conditions

Homemade Shampoo (Includes 34 Organic Shampoo Recipes!)

Homemade Makeup (Includes 28 Organic Makeup Recipes!)

Homemade Deodorant (Includes 20 Organic Deodorant Recipes!)

Homemade Lip Balm (Includes 22 Organic Lip Balm Recipes!)

Homemade Bath Salts (Includes 35 Organic Bath Salt Recipes!)

(All books available as digital downloads and printed books)